ACCEL
LE
Pocketbook

D0865831

By Brin Best

Cartoons:
Phil Hailstone

Published by:

Teachers' Pocketbooks
Laurel House, Station Approach,
Alresford, Hampshire SO24 9JH, UK
Tel: +44 (0)1962 735573
Fax: +44 (0)1962 733637
E-mail: sales@teacherspocketbooks.co.uk
Website: www.teacherspocketbooks.co.uk

*Teachers' Pocketbooks is an imprint of
Management Pocketbooks Ltd.*

This edition published 2003.
Reprinted 2004, 2005, 2006.

ISBN 13 – 978 1 930776 53 7
ISBN 10   1 903776 53 8

British Library Cataloguing-in-Publication
Data – A catalogue record for this book is
available from the British Library.

Design, typesetting and graphics by Efex Ltd.
Printed in UK.

Contents

Introduction

How to use this Pocketbook

This book is about how to teach in a way that maximises your students' chances of reaching their potential. It provides a range of practical, tried and tested strategies and techniques that have been shown to get results. But, be warned – you must be prepared to have your beliefs on effective methods of teaching challenged!

Accelerated learning happens when teachers take account of how our brains learn most effectively. It is based on recent research into the physiology of the brain and on studies into the most effective teaching methods from around the world. Teachers who have used these methods are getting spectacular results in their classrooms, with their students becoming more motivated and engaged in their learning.

Over the last few decades we have taken a huge leap forward in our understanding of the brain and how people learn. Although there is much still to find out, what we already know has allowed us to devise a powerful range of methods that are set to revolutionise teaching. Although many of these have been used by teachers in a less structured way for years, we now have a growing body of evidence to back up these methods.

How to use this Pocketbook

The aim of this book is to draw together in a handy, pocket-sized format all the information you need to take advantage of the accelerated learning methods in your classroom. Within these pages you will find a wealth of advice that, if implemented with commitment, will result in the kind of engagement in learning that so many teachers are looking for. It will also help your students **learn how to learn**, enabling them to become lifelong learners and achieve success in the changing world of tomorrow.

Towards the end of the book is a **self-evaluation framework** that will help you to judge how far along the continuum of accelerated learning you have reached in your own classroom. It will also allow you to record what needs to be done for you to progress to the next level.

Embracing the principles of accelerated learning means that you must model these principles as you work, in order to become an **accelerated learner** yourself. This book is based on these principles in the way it is written, its structure and design. Overleaf you will find a list of ways to ensure you are an accelerated learner as you use it.

Being an accelerated learner as you use the book

- Jot down what you already know about accelerated learning (this activates your **prior knowledge**)
- Make a note of what you want to get out of reading this book (these are your **learning goals**)
- Make sure you are in the right **physical** and **emotional state** to learn
- Skim through the book first to get the **big picture**

Being an accelerated learner as you use the book

- As you read, highlight sections, underline key words, and jot down any questions that come to mind (this will increase your **interaction** with the book)
- Take **'brain breaks'** as you work to give your brain a rest and the chance to assimilate what you have learnt (eg: 'brain gym', page 33)
- Carry out any exercises or tasks suggested in the book so your learning is **active**
- Tell others about what you have learnt (thereby **demonstrating** you have learnt it)
- Complete the self-evaluation section at the back so you have a series of action points to tackle that can form the basis of your **accelerated learning development plan**
- **Put into action** your development plan, involving other people along the way to help you make it a success
- **Review** the contents of the book at regular intervals so the key information is transferred to your long-term memory, **testing** yourself as you do so

Classroom changes since the Victorian era

To help illustrate the principles of accelerated learning we shall begin with a table comparing three classrooms in the UK, each from a different decade in the last hundred years.

Feature	Example A	Example B	Example C
Class size	Very large (often over 40)	Large (often over 30)	Small (never more than 30)
Seating arrangements	Students seated in rows behind desks	Students seated in rows behind desks	Students seated at computer workstations or behind desks arranged in more creative patterns
Teacher's equipment	Slate and chalk	Blackboard and chalk	Whiteboard or interactive whiteboard linked to computer
Where students' work is recorded	On slates	In exercise books	Saved on disk or in mind-maps as well as traditional forms of recording on paper

Feature	Example A	Example B	Example C
Style of learning	Rote learning and repetition; every student does the same work	Much rote learning and repetition; every student does the same work, in preferred learning style of teacher	A variety of learning opportunities offered according to students' preferred learning styles; students can choose tasks
Classroom climate	High stress; use of physical punishments commonplace for poor performance	High stress; extensive use of put downs and threats of punishment to get control	Low stress; supportive approaches used, with much negotiation
Thinking skills	Absent	Rarely encountered	Embedded into teaching
View of intelligence	Viewed as genetically determined	Viewed as fixed and based on measures of IQ	Viewed as flexible and belonging to one of many different intelligences
Inclusion	Teaching not inclusive (eg: weak students wear dunce's hat); those with barriers to learning not taught	Teaching beginning to be inclusive (eg: some work differentiated); many students with barriers to learning educated separately	Inclusive, with individuals' barriers to learning addressed; support assistants used to help individuals overcome barriers

Now try this task before turning over: estimate to the nearest decade which dates these classrooms refer to and write the date in pencil at the top of each column.

Classroom changes since the Victorian era

The answer to the question on the previous page is as follows (correct the answers you put if you were wrong!)

Classroom A – 1900   Classroom B – 1980   Classroom C – 2000

The important points here are that:

- By the 1980s we still had an essentially **Victorian** model for our education system in this country, particularly with respect to the way students were taught and treated

- Example C may not resemble your classroom! It is an **accelerated learning classroom** and most closely resembles the UK's most advanced accelerated learning school at Cramlington Community High School, Northumberland (see page 119 for details of Wise and Lovatt, 2001). Many classrooms elsewhere in the country in the year 2000 still retained features of the 1980s (and hence the Victorian) model

This book is about how you can move your classroom towards the kind of model described in example C.

Why do we need accelerated learning?

A crucial point about the accelerated learning approaches outlined in this book is that they are based on very sound **scientific evidence** on how the brain works and people learn. But this evidence has only been available for a few decades.

Since the early 1900s many crucial scientific discoveries changed the face of medicine, so much so that the type of hospital ward which existed then can no longer be found in this country. This is in marked contrast to the continued existence of the essentially **Victorian classroom** in which we still educate our young people, as the previous examples showed.

Now that we have the knowledge needed radically to **improve** the way we teach, we must take advantage of it, as the early medical pioneers did to improve the health and quality of life of so many of our ancestors. *The Accelerated Learning Pocketbook* is your guide to beginning that revolution in your classroom.

Accelerated learning in a nutshell

Here is the 'big picture' showing you how to create an accelerated learning lesson:

1. Ensure your students are in the correct **physical state** to learn (proper hydration and nourishment are important, as are room temperature and oxygen levels)
2. Use **music in a structured way**
3. Help students enter a positive **emotional state** for learning
4. Create an **environment that supports learning** but make activities challenging
5. Develop **good working relationships** with your students and use praise frequently
6. Plan **inclusive learning activities** that respect the full range of learning styles and intelligences, and are **accessible** to all students

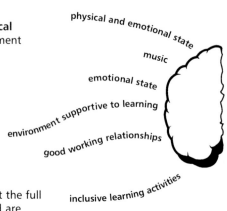

physical and emotional state

music

emotional state

environment supportive to learning

good working relationships

inclusive learning activities

Accelerated learning in a nutshell (cont'd)

7. Include this **sequence** in lessons (see pages 49-52 for details):
   Part 1: put the learning in context   Part 2: starter
   Part 3: main teaching and learning   Part 4: plenary

8. Allow **breaks** for light physical activity (eg: 'brain gym', p. 33)

9. Use a **variety of teaching methods**, including thinking skills and visual tools to develop higher order skills

10. Make **learning skills** such as mind-mapping and memory techniques part of your lesson

11. Encourage students to **review** their own progress and set personal goals

12. **Evaluate** your lesson in consultation with your students

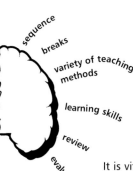

It is vital to appreciate that the most effective learning occurs when **all**, or as many as possible, of these elements are **combined** in your lessons. Simply turning on music or getting students to drink water or draw mind maps will not result in accelerated learning in itself, and you must place great emphasis on the actual **teaching strategies** you use in your lessons.

How realistic are the methods in this book?

For some readers, the methods outlined in this book may seem over-ambitious, inappropriate for their school, or downright impractical. However, they are based on solid evidence of how to accelerate learning and case studies from the author's own completely standard comprehensive school, as well as findings from schools in a variety of settings across the country and overseas.

Some of these schools are located in the most socially deprived communities in England, others are in the more leafy suburbs, or in remote countryside. What has united the teachers in these schools is their **commitment** to implementing the methods and **belief** that they *will* make a difference.

Whatever type of school you work in you *can* successfully introduce all the techniques described in this book if you feel strongly enough about it – but you can't introduce them all overnight!

Overcoming barriers to implementation in your school

It can be difficult to keep your nerve if you are the only teacher in your school prepared to introduce the accelerated learning methods, especially if most of your colleagues are traditional in their approach, or resistant to change. **Take heart** from the following findings from schools that have successfully introduced the methods:

- Once students have experienced the methods with one teacher, they often become powerful advocates for the introduction of the methods to their other lessons
- Teachers who have been teaching for over 20 years have found the techniques just as helpful as have those new to the profession
- OFSTED inspectors are increasingly making positive reference to accelerated learning in their reports on schools
- Cramlington Community High School (the most advanced school in the country in implementing the accelerated learning methods) took four years to introduce the methods to all departments – take things one step at a time

Notes

Getting your Students Ready to Learn

The amazing brain

The brain is the most **complicated** organ that we possess, and there is still much we do not understand about how it works and how it allows us to function as complex humans.

But in the last few decades brain scientists have taken great strides forward in their understanding of many of the important aspects of brain function, including how we learn. Advanced imaging techniques have, for the first time, allowed us to actually see what is happening as we learn.

Slowly, a picture of the geography of the brain has emerged that identifies which parts of it are responsible for different functions. Knowledge of these regions has been helpful in allowing us to understand how we perceive the world, and process this information to learn.

Three types of brain

It is sometimes helpful to think of the brain as actually three types of brain in one, although most brain scientists now think you can't physically separate the brain in these ways:

- The **reptilian** brain responsible for fight or flight responses
- The **mammalian** brain or limbic system, which controls emotions and long-term memory
- The **neocortex** which is involved in intellectual thinking and problem solving

The brain contains billions of structures called **neurons** which connect together to create an incredibly complicated network along which signals are transmitted.

In times of **stress** your brain enters its 'reptilian state' when the priority is to meet its immediate needs. During these times it may be physically *impossible* to learn.

Two hemispheres of the brain?

The traditional model of the brain depicts two **hemispheres** which have different roles in helping you make sense of the world:

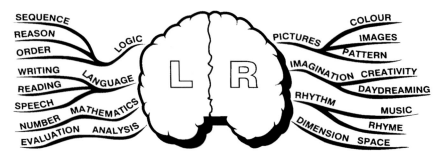

Modern neuroscientists argue that this is far too **simplistic** a representation, and the concept of lateralisation is out of date. They favour the view that the brain carries out a wide range of functions as listed in the diagram, but the precise centres where processing occurs are not yet fully understood.

Brain states

Every second our brains generate minute electrical impulses. Scientists who have attached sensitive electrodes to people's scalps have discovered that brains emit four different types of electrical signals, or '**brain waves**'.

Beta: characterising the conscious mind: you are wide awake and figuring out complex problems

Alpha: characterises relaxation and meditation and facilitates inspiration, fast assimilation of facts and heightened memory. This is the ideal state for the kind of learning that goes on in classrooms

Theta: characterising deep relaxation, where flashes of inspiration can occur

Delta: characterising deep dreamless sleep

Alpha brain waves are best for learning

At any one time there will be a mixture of different wave types being emitted, but one type will tend to dominate, which is used to describe the **brain state** people are in.

Scientific experiments have shown that the *alpha* wave state is the most conducive for learning, and the search is on for ways to get learners into that state and keep them in it throughout the learning experience. You can help your students enter the alpha state by relaxation exercises and activities such as brain gym (page 33).

Good nutrition

We now realise that the brain, rather like any other organ, needs to be specifically **nurtured** in order for it to be in tip-top condition to carry out its key functions.

What we eat has an important effect on the brain's ability to function properly. In particular, it is vital to maintain a healthy and balanced diet that, as well as keeping your body fit and healthy, will supply you with **vitamins A, B, C and E**. These vitamins play a role in staying alert, vision, memory and proper brain function in general.

Too much sugar, starch, caffeine and other unnecessary drugs can impair mental function. Make sure your students understand the importance of good nutrition, in particular a good breakfast to get them ready for a day of learning. Some schools have successfully introduced 'breakfast clubs' which have proved highly popular.

Encourage your students to eat regularly and not to skip any meals, as the brain needs a steady supply of energy.

The importance of water

The brain needs to be well **hydrated** to work properly. Dehydration can lead to lethargy and lack of concentration. The brain is in a dehydrated state before you notice the physical signs of dehydration, such as a dry mouth or a headache.

Schools that have actively encouraged their students to drink water have been impressed with the improvements in concentration and behaviour that have resulted. It also results in fewer interruptions, as students do not need to ask to go out for a drink any more.

Contrary to what you might think, after a few weeks' adjustment the students do not continually have to go to the toilet during their lessons! In fact by drinking more water students will develop more healthy urinary systems, and water has been shown to have many other health benefits.

The importance of water

Points to bear in mind when introducing water into your classroom:

- Explain to your students **why** you are introducing water and **how** it can help them
- Consider providing **water dispensers** in the corridor and allow each student to bring their own **water bottle** into the classroom
- To minimise spillages you may want to stop for **water breaks** every so often
- Encourage your students to **visit the toilet during breaks** and, when possible, before the lesson begins, to avoid interruptions during the lesson
- Some teachers are very reluctant to allow water into their classrooms but it soon becomes an **everyday part** of the students' equipment, along with their pencil-case and exercise books
- Do not allow **sugary or fizzy drinks** into the classroom – these can have undesirable side effects for learning as well as being messy (see next page)
- In some classroom environments, such as science laboratories, it may not be **appropriate** for students to drink – instead take water breaks in the corridor
- If you let your students drink water as they work, you soon find out how much they appreciate it – small things can make a real difference

What learners shouldn't drink

Young people (and adults) habitually consume drinks that can actually **hinder** learning.

- Fizzy pop contains huge amounts of sugar (up to 12 teaspoons per can) and caffeine
- Many fruit squashes contain large amounts of added sugar
- Tea and coffee are high in caffeine and sugar is frequently added to them

Taking in extra sugar may give your students an initial rush, but this is quickly replaced by increased lethargy.

Caffeine is a drug which impairs brain function as well as leading to increased headaches. Teachers take note!

The correct temperature for learning

The brain needs to be **neither too cool nor too warm** in order to function best, but the optimal temperature probably varies from one individual to another.

If the temperature is too hot your students will soon feel lethargic and be in danger of dehydration. If the temperature is too cold then they will be concentrating on ways to get warm rather than what you want them to learn! You should allow students to move around a classroom to discover the most comfortable working temperature for them and encourage them to put on/take off a layer if they are cold/warm.

Controlling the temperature in your classroom can be tricky, as many schools' heating systems are notoriously unreliable and outdated. You may wish to liaise with your on-site staff and senior management team in order to have better control over the temperature in your classroom. Make sure you have a **thermometer** in your classroom so you can judge the temperature accurately.

Oxygen and light levels

When your students begin to yawn a lot this is a sure sign that there is not enough **oxygen** in your classroom. Oxygen is absolutely vital to effective brain function.

You can increase the amount of oxygen in your classroom by:

- Opening a window to allow fresh air in
- Opening your door
- Introducing plants into your classroom (this has other benefits too, page 44)

There should also be as much **natural light** in your classroom as possible, as this is thought to promote concentration and learning. Some studies have suggested that standard bulbs are preferable to fluorescent lighting if you have an option.

Stress levels

We are living in times of record **stress levels** among young people. This is worrying for teachers, as stress can impair brain function to the extent that no learning is possible.

It is vital that your students understand the link between stress and learning, and that your school has an active programme in place to help them reduce their stress levels. In your classroom there are a number of ways (see next page) in which you can help your students rid themselves of negative stress levels.

Stress levels

How to reduce student stress levels:

- **Acknowledge** at the start of the lesson that some students may not be entering the lesson in the best state to learn because of heightened stress
- Use the **traffic light** approach – ask students to hold up one of three coloured cards (green, amber or red) to indicate how ready to learn they feel
- Introduce **relaxing music** into your lesson to greet the students (see pages 42-43)
- Experiment with **meditation** and relaxation exercises
- Many schools are finding '**brain gym**' (light physical activity linked to the cross-connection of the two brain hemispheres) very helpful – see next page

Many of the exercises listed above will help your students to access the alpha state, the state of relaxed alertness that is the ideal state for learning.

Brain gym

Brain gym is being enthusiastically taken up by many schools as a starter activity before learning begins, or to be used during a 'brain break'. Students enjoy brain gym, even after the initial novelty has worn off and most do find it genuinely beneficial in getting them in the alpha state to learn.

Here are two brain gym exercises you can try:

- Rub tummy and pat head at the same time.
- Draw figures of eight with your finger in the air, first with one hand, then the other, then both together. If this is easy, start drawing from the opposite end!

For further details of brain gym activities, see the websites mentioned on page 124.

Motivation

Your students will not learn effectively if they lack the **motivation** to learn.
There are two forms of motivation:

- **Intrinsic motivation** – that which comes from within the individual, emanating from a desire to succeed at a particular task

- **Extrinsic motivation** – this is motivation from outside the individual, such as that provided by a reward or the threat of a sanction

It is important to try to move your students towards intrinsic motivation, so that they feel compelled to learn even if the external motivation is taken away.

The techniques included in this book make learning much more **engaging** and **enjoyable**. Many teachers have found that by introducing the methods into their classrooms, levels of behaviour and motivation improve dramatically. Success leads to motivation and accelerated learning certainly results in successful learners.

Developing intrinsic motivation

Although you should accept that some students have a natural liking for a subject you do not teach, there are specific **strategies and techniques** that can be used to develop intrinsic motivation.

- Encourage your students to consider what benefits there might be from learning your subject and how it could help them later in their lives – ie: what's in it for them?

- Ask your students to set their own learning goals – having a goal for learning increases levels of engagement and motivation, providing it is a realistic one.

The importance of sleep

Deep, restful **sleep** is emerging as an important factor in effective learning.
This may be because one of the primary functions of sleep is for the brain to process
and make sense of what has been learnt during the day. Contrary to what you might
think, your brain is actually still quite active as you sleep.

This is backed up by studies that have shown that the more people are deprived of
sleep, the less they remember of what they have studied during the day. It is also
noteworthy that young children, who are learning so much new about the world,
need more sleep than adults.

Although encouraging your students to get a good night's sleep may seem more like
the kind of advice their parents might give, there is good evidence to suggest it makes
sense if they want to learn effectively. Different people seem to need slightly different
amounts of sleep, but surveys routinely show that many people are getting an hour or
so less per night than they ideally need.

Introduction

 Getting your Students Ready to Learn

 Creating the Right Environment ◀

 Teaching Strategies

 Self-evaluation Framework

 Further Information

Creating the Right Environment

A classroom for learning

Your classroom should be a **multi-sensory environment** where learning is easy. But this will not happen by accident – you have to create that environment.

The importance of displays

Every classroom has plenty of space available for **displays**, but do you use the wall space in your classroom effectively? Use the walls of your classroom to display:

- Students' work, including examples from individuals with different abilities
- Students' work to illustrate specific levels or grades
- Posters about the topics your students are learning
- Motivational posters
- Key words about specific topics you are teaching
- Photographs of students enjoying their learning, to generate a positive attitude

Make sure that all displays are **updated** frequently. This is a task that you can get enthusiastic students to take charge of.

Seating arrangements can support learning

Make sure the arrangement of desks supports the activity you wish to undertake. For the majority of classroom activities the **horseshoe** shape is the most flexible.

The advantages of the horseshoe shape are:

- It allows maximum interaction between students during discussions
- It permits easy access by the teacher to all students
- It ensures the teacher can see all students' faces at all times

Seating arrangements can support learning

Some classrooms are obviously easier to rearrange than others (eg: science labs). In these cases be creative with where students sit, eg: with group discussion or demonstrations held at the front of the class, ask students to bring their stools with them in order to participate.

Experiment with different layouts to determine the most suitable ones for your needs and encourage students to change places on a regular basis, as they will gain from interacting with new neighbours.

Using music to aid learning

Music can be used in a variety of ways to aid the learning process. The use of music burst into the educational arena in the 1990s with the so-called 'Mozart effect' – a temporary improvement in performance in spatial-temporal reasoning by college students who were played the first ten minutes of a Mozart sonata.

Although other researches have failed fully to replicate this specific effect in more recent studies, there is now general acceptance that music can aid the learning process in several different ways. The benefits are certainly not solely associated with baroque music.

It is also worth bearing in mind that if you ask your students, almost all of them will say they prefer to listen to music when working at home. The silent classroom traditionally enjoyed by many teachers and seen as a sign of control is not the environment your students would choose to work in. To some students the silence can even be unsettling.

Using music to aid learning

Here are some specific ways to use music in your classroom:

- Use **upbeat, positive** music to greet students and set the tone for the lesson
- When studying a particular **country or culture**, use appropriate music to support the lesson (eg: a South African choir when studying apartheid, blues music when studying the black history of the USA, the Beatles when studying an aspect of Liverpool)
- Use **relaxing** music (such as *Enya*) to help your students get in the alpha brain state ready to learn – this should have a rhythm which is as close to sixty beats per minute as possible
- Play relaxing **background music** when your students work (there is room for negotiation here over the type of music your students enjoy)
- Use **dramatic music** during a review at the end of your lesson (sometimes called the 'concert review')

Remember that having music in your classroom isn't simply a matter of turning on the radio as a treat – its use needs to be carefully thought out and music selected that is appropriate to the task.

Plants

Several studies have linked the presence of **plants** and other **nature** in classrooms with improved performance and lower stress levels. The specific benefits of plants include their ability to:

- Oxygenate a room
- Filter out harmful gases from the air, including those from computer equipment
- Create a calming atmosphere
- Provide a point of interest during a lesson

Some teachers are also discovering the benefits of introducing fish into their classrooms, or other pets. **Fish** seem to be particularly good at creating a relaxed atmosphere, for reasons which are currently unclear.

Research is ongoing into the beneficial effects of nature in classrooms. It is of related interest too that contact with animals and plants seems to help people with illnesses recover more quickly.

Creating an environment that supports learning

It is vital that you cultivate a **supportive learning environment** in your classroom so that every student feels secure, comfortable and ready to learn. In particular it is important that:

- There are clear **classroom rules** which have been negotiated with the students and focus on what everyone can do to help others to learn
- Students have the opportunity to say what they expect from the **teacher**
- There are consistently **high expectations** in line with the abilities of individuals
- **Mistakes** when learning are tolerated or even encouraged
- The **views of everyone** are listened to and matter
- There are **no personal put-downs** or insults
- **Praise** is given frequently to individuals and groups
- The teacher is not always seen as having the '**right**' answer

How students can support each other

Students play a key role in creating and maintaining a supportive learning environment for their peers. Explain to your students the need for everyone to work together harmoniously, and insist that all your students know the consequences if they do not do this.

If you **cultivate** an atmosphere where unhelpful behaviour is not seen as part of your classroom, high standards of behaviour soon become expected. Having a clear list of sanctions can also help students to understand the consequences of their behaviour. This should end with removal from the classroom, which should be seen as the ultimate sanction, as the students are not benefiting from your help directly as they learn.

Introduction

 Getting your
Students Ready
to Learn

 Creating the
Right
Environment

 Teaching
Strategies

 Self-evaluation
Framework

 Further
Information

Teaching
Strategies

Before the lessons begins

The beginnings of lessons are vital because they help set the tone for the rest of the lesson. Ensure you:

- **Arrive before the students** to give preparation time
- **Greet each student** politely and in a friendly way
- **Insist students enter quietly** and settle at their desks in an orderly fashion
- Consider using **music** to set the tone for the lesson
- Make sure any **equipment** and **handouts** are ready to give out, and on the students' desk if appropriate
- **Engage students' interest** with a question or puzzle on the board

Structuring a lesson

It is important that you provide an effective structure for all your lessons that promotes your students' learning. The following provides a 'brain-friendly' 4-part structure for your lessons.

Part 1: put the learning in context (about 5% of lesson time)

- Explore what the students learnt in the previous lesson
- Relate the learning to the overall syllabus
- Make the learning outcomes clear
- Explain what is coming in the next lesson
- Mind-maps can be a very useful visual tool for this part of the lesson, showing students how an individual lesson fits into the wider course they are studying

Structuring a lesson

Part 2: starter (about 10% of lesson time)

- Begin with a short activity which engages students' interest – a prop, story, exciting stimulus material
- Try to help students put what they already know about the topic in context
- Prepare the students for the main teaching and learning that will follow

Structuring a lesson

Part 3: main teaching and learning (about 75% of lesson time)

- Students should be carrying out activities for as much of this time as possible
- You should act as a facilitator for their learning – try not to talk for too long
- Students should be engaged in multi-sensory learning that respects their learning styles and intelligence profiles
- All students should be set work which is of an appropriate level of challenge
- Allow choice over how students carry out tasks
- Learning should be broken down into achievable chunks
- Find plenty of opportunities to develop thinking skills

Structuring a lesson

Part 4: plenary (about 10% of lesson time)

- Provides an opportunity for learning to be reviewed
- Students should be given the chance to reflect on what they think the main learning points of the lesson have been
- You should include careful use of teacher questioning (see next page)

part **1** — Put the learning in context

part **2** — Starter

part **3** — Main teaching and learning

part **4** — Plenary

This 4-part structure is adapted from the one used in the **Key Stage 3 strategy**.

Questioning

Effective questioning techniques are a really important part of your lesson. Questioning helps you determine how much your students have understood, as well as allowing you to stretch more able students.

- Use a **wide range** of questioning techniques
- Pitch the **language** and **content level** of questions appropriately
- Ask **open** as well as closed questions to explore deeper understanding
- **Prompt** and **give clues** where necessary
- Allow **thinking time** (at least five seconds for simple questions and ten seconds or more for more complex ones)
- **Invite answers** from particular individuals as well as asking the whole class
- **Wait before commenting** on a student's answers, thereby allowing him/her to revise or expand their response, and encouraging others to contribute too
- **Do not favour** students with higher ability or according to where they are seated (you will tend to neglect those closest to you and those right at the back of the room)
- Encourage students to **devise their own questions**

Varying your teaching style

The most successful teachers use an extensive **repertoire** of different teaching techniques to stimulate interest among their students. Providing variety will help increase your students' motivation. Use the checklist below to help you vary your teaching style.

Reflect back over the last half-term and indicate with a tick whether your students have:

☐ Used a newspaper
☐ Played a game
☐ Answered questions from a book
☐ Had a discussion
☐ Made a model
☐ Done a quiz or test
☐ Written an essay
☐ Written a newspaper article
☐ Worked in a pair or a group
☐ Had a debate
☐ Done a role play
☐ Made up a play or a TV/radio script

☐ Done some individual or group research
☐ Done some extended reading
☐ Done a brainstorming session
☐ Drawn a graph or used statistics
☐ Drawn a diagram or cartoon
☐ Used music in their work
☐ Been outside the classroom for a task or activity
☐ Worked with an outside speaker
☐ Sat in different places from usual
☐ Worked in the school library
☐ Worked on a poster
☐ Worked with somebody they don't know very well

Student tasks

Tips for explaining and introducing tasks:

- Always give the tasks verbally **and** in writing to include different types of learners
- **Make sure that all students understand** what they have to do
- **Carefully differentiate all tasks** to ensure all students can achieve success
- **Chunk down** new information and tasks to make them more accessible
- **Give a time frame** for the tasks to help students manage their own learning

Student tasks

Tips for setting tasks:

- Where possible, **offer choice** in the tasks undertaken or the way the results are presented
- **Include a wide variety of tasks** that appeal to different types of learners and different intelligences
- **Allow plenty of opportunity for pair work and group work**, as well as individual work

Student tasks

Tips for when students are working:

- **Circulate widely** to check they are on task, progressing well and finding appropriate answers

- **Do not insist that students work in silence** as long as their talk is focused on the tasks

- Try to maximise the amount of time when students are **carrying out** and **reflecting** on tasks

Showing what students have learnt

It is important to give your students opportunities to show what they have learnt. This can be done by students:

- **Checking** their own written responses
- **Reading out** their responses to others for discussion
- Giving **presentations** to the class
- **Completing** tests, quizzes and mind-maps

Students also demonstrate their knowledge in their written work, allowing you to give constructive feedback and judge how they are progressing.

Review

Students need plenty of opportunities to **review** what they have learnt, for example by:

- Writing out summary points
- Drawing a mind-map of a lesson or topic
- Naming the most important thing learnt from a lesson
- Preparing flashcards or summary diagrams

Review is also an essential element of **revision** for tests and formal examinations. It transfers information to the long-term memory, particularly if done a week, a month and six months after first studied.

Make sure at the **end** of every lesson there is an activity which sums up what has been learnt and prepares the students for the next lesson. This could take place as part of a **plenary**, which is a key feature of the **Key Stage 3 strategy**.

Homework

Homework is a valuable way of extending accelerated learning beyond the classroom, providing the opportunity for a range of tasks to be carried out which help embed learning.

Homework is **effective** when:

- It is used to extend and enrich learning
- It builds on what has been learnt in the lesson
- It takes advantages of the opportunities in the students' home lives, eg: parents/carers, grandparents, local features of interest
- It is enjoyable

Homework should **not** be:

- Simply finishing off work done in lessons
- Optional
- Given only to those who work hard
- Given only to those who do not finish a piece of work in class

Learners with different learning styles

The brain receives information about the world through the five senses or 'channels':

- Sight (the visual channel)
- Touch (the kinaesthetic channel)
- Sound (the auditory channel)
- Taste (the gustatory channel)
- Smell (the olfactory channel)

Studies of how we learn have identified three primary channels through which learning occurs: **auditory**, **kinaesthetic** and **visual**.

However, not all individuals prefer to learn through the same combination of channels, and for most people a single one tends to dominate. This has given rise to an exciting development in teaching and learning where individuals' preferred **learning styles** are assessed and used to create richer and more inclusive learning experiences (see www.support4learning.org.uk for examples of learning style questionnaires).

The most powerful learning takes place when **all three channels** are used simultaneously.

Characteristics of auditory learners

Approximately 34% of people have an **auditory** learning preference. They tend to have the following characteristics:

- They use phrases such as 'that **sounds** right', 'I **hear** what you are saying', 'That **rings** a bell'
- When relaxing, they prefer to listen to music
- They prefer to talk to people on the phone
- They enjoy listening to others, but are eager to talk themselves
- They forget faces but remember names
- When inactive, they tend to talk to themselves or others
- When angry, they express themselves in outbursts
- They are not fond of reading books or instruction manuals

Learning activities for auditory learners

The following activities are suitable for learners with an **auditory** learning preference:

- Hearing a presentation or explanation
- Reading aloud to themselves
- Making a tape of key points to listen to
- Verbally summarising in their own words
- Explaining the subject to another student
- Using their own internal voice to verbalise what they are learning
- Practising spellings by saying the correct word before trying to write it

Characteristics of kinaesthetic learners

Approximately 37% of people have a **kinaesthetic** learning preference. They tend to have the following characteristics:

- They use phrases such as 'That **feels** right', 'I found it easy to **handle**', 'That **touched** a nerve'
- When relaxing, they prefer to play games and sport
- They prefer to talk to people while doing something else
- They are slow talkers, who use gestures and expressions
- When inactive, they tend to fidget
- When angry, they clench their fists, grit their teeth and storm off!

Learning activities for kinaesthetic learners

The following activities are suitable for learners with a **kinaesthetic** learning preference:

- Copying demonstrations
- Making models
- Recording information as they hear it, preferably in a mind-map
- Walking around as they read
- Underlining/highlighting new information/key points
- Putting key points on to index cards and sorting them into order
- Getting physically and actively involved in learning
- Practising spellings by writing with a finger in the air or on the desk, while simultaneously saying it aloud

Characteristics of visual learners

Approximately 29% of people have a **visual** learning preference. They tend to have the following characteristics:

- They use phrases such as 'I **see** what you mean', 'I get the **picture**, 'That **looks** right'
- When relaxing, they prefer to watch a film or video, go to the theatre or read a book
- They prefer to talk to people face-to-face
- They are fast talkers and do not enjoy listening to others
- They forget names, but remember faces
- When inactive, they tend to doodle or watch someone or something
- When angry they are silent and seethe
- They are well dressed, tidy and organised

Learning activities for visual learners

The following activities are suitable for learners with a **visual** learning preference:

- Writing down key facts or drawing a mind-map
- Visualising what they are learning
- Creating pictures/diagrams from what they are learning
- Using time lines, for remembering dates
- Creating their own strong visual links
- Using pictures, diagrams, charts, film, video and graphics
- Practising spellings by seeing the word before writing or saying it

The information on different learning styles on the previous pages is based on material that first appeared in *The Learner's Pocketbook* by Paul Hayden.

Two types of processing

Learners also tend to prefer to **process** information in one of two ways:

● **Wholists** – they process information in wholes
● **Analysts** – they process information in parts

It is a good thing for all your students to process the information in different ways, to help them gain a deeper understanding of it.

A word of caution
Some education professionals have expressed concern over schools that use analysis of students' learning styles to determine a rather narrow approach to teaching. Try to ensure that learners of all types are included in learning experiences, but encourage individuals to learn in ways which may not come naturally to them. This increases their **learning repertoire**.

Recognising the multiple intelligences

Until the 1980s intelligence was generally viewed as fixed and was measured using the standard intelligence quotient test. University of Harvard professor Howard Gardner changed the way we looked at intelligence with his highly influential work on **multiple intelligences** summarised in his book *Frames of mind: the theory of multiple intelligences* (1993).

According to Gardner's theory there are eight types of intelligence:

- **Bodily kinaesthetic intelligence** – used for touch and reflex
- **Inter-personal intelligence** – used for communicating with others
- **Intra-personal intelligence** – used for self-discovery and analysis
- **Linguistic intelligence** – used for reading, writing and speech
- **Logical mathematical intelligence** – used for maths, logic and systems
- **Musical intelligence** – used for rhythm, music and lyrics
- **Naturalistic intelligence** – used for making sense of the natural world
- **Visual spatial intelligence** – used for visualisation and art

Recognising the multiple intelligences

Everybody possesses all **eight** intelligences to some extent and the most powerful learning combines all eight. All the intelligences have value and it is important to identify your students' strengths and weaknesses to make the most of these, as well as noting areas for further development.

The theory of multiple intelligences is very helpful for a number of reasons:

- It means that every one of your students can find out in **which ways they are intelligent**, rather than discovering **how intelligent** they are
- It supports **inclusion** by making it clear that people have many individual strengths and weaknesses
- It allows us to view intelligence as a **broader concept** than simply the ability to be successful in an IQ test

Bodily kinaesthetic intelligence

Used for touch and reflex

An individual with well-developed **bodily kinaesthetic** intelligence tends to have the following characteristics and likes:

Characteristics
- Often good at sport
- Never sits still
- Fidgets
- Mechanically minded
- Likes to touch
- Solves problems physically ('hands on')
- Good with their hands
- Controlled reflexes
- Control of body
- Control of objects
- Good timing

Likes
- Sport/games
- Rough and tumble play
- Acting and drama
- Dancing
- Cooking
- Handicrafts
- DIY

Learning activities for bodily kinaesthetic intelligence

- Learn by doing
- Role play and drama
- Field trips
- Physical involvement in the subject
- Taking action, eg: writing down points or mind-mapping
- Making models
- Card-sorting exercises
- Moving about while working
- Changing activity frequently
- Mental review of learning while doing physical exercise

Inter-personal intelligence

Used for communicating with others

An individual with well-developed **inter-personal** intelligence tends to have the following characteristics and likes:

Characteristics
- Relates to and mixes well with others
- Puts people at ease
- Has numerous friends
- Sympathetic to others' feelings
- Mediates between people in dispute
- Good communicator
- Good at negotiating
- Co-operative

Likes
- Being with people
- Social events and community activities
- Clubs
- Group activities/team tasks
- Taking charge of others

Learning activities for inter-personal intelligence

- Learning from others
- Working in teams
- Talking to others to get and share answers
- Comparing notes after a study session
- Making use of mentoring
- Teaching others

Intra-personal intelligence

Used for self-discovery and analysis

An individual with well-developed **intra-personal** intelligence tends to have the following characteristics and likes:

Characteristics
- Understands own feelings and behaviour
- Self-intuitive, knows own strengths
- Private
- Independent
- Wants to be different from the crowd
- Keeps a diary/journal
- Plans time effectively
- Self-motivated
- Sets and achieves goals

Likes
- Peace and quiet
- Day-dreaming
- Reflecting/reminiscing
- Independence
- Achieving goals
- Own company

Learning activities for intra-personal intelligence

- Using personal affirmations
- Setting goals and targets for learning
- Creating personal interest in the learning
- Taking control of learning
- Carrying out independent learning
- Seeking out the human angle
- Listening to intuition
- Reflecting, writing or discussing what was experienced and the feelings this invoked
- Reflecting on how information fits in with existing knowledge and experiences

Linguistic intelligence

Used for reading, writing and speech

An individual with well-developed **linguistic** intelligence tends to have the following characteristics and likes:

Characteristics
- Extensive vocabulary
- Good at spelling
- Good verbal and/or written communication
- Expressive fluent talker
- Good listener
- Gives clear explanations
- Strong reasoning ability
- Methodical

Likes
- Reading
- Word games/crosswords
- Theatre
- Poetry
- Debate
- Radio
- Writing letters

Learning activities for linguistic intelligence

- Learning from books, tapes, lectures, presentations
- Writing down questions that need to be answered before starting to learn
- Reading aloud
- After reading a piece of text, summarising in own words out loud and writing this down
- Putting things in own words
- Brainstorming to organise thoughts into order or to distinguish key points
- Making up crosswords and puzzles to solve
- Debating and discussing issues
- Presenting what has been learnt orally or in writing to another student

Logical mathematical intelligence

Used for maths, logic and systems

An individual with well-developed **logical mathematical** intelligence tends to have the following characteristics and likes:

Characteristics
- Good at budgeting
- Logical thought, explanation and action
- Organised
- Organises tasks into sequence
- Plans time effectively
- Reasons effectively
- Seeks patterns and relationships
- Precise

Likes
- Calculations
- Solving puzzles
- Abstract thought
- Experimenting
- Science
- ICT

Learning activities for logical mathematical intelligence

- Listing key points in order and numbering them
- Using a flowchart to express information/knowledge in easy-to-follow steps
- Using mind-maps
- Using computers, eg: spreadsheets
- Experimenting with knowledge
- Using timelines for remembering dates and events
- Analysing and interpreting data
- Using reasoning and deductive skills
- Creating and solving problems
- Playing mathematical games

Musical intelligence

Used for rhythm, music and lyrics

An individual with well-developed **musical** intelligence tends to have the following characteristics and likes:

Characteristics
- Sensitive to pitch, rhythm and timbre
- Sensitive to emotion of music
- Changes mood with music
- Good at clapping in time to music
- Remembers and repeats slogans and lyrics easily
- Good at selecting background music
- May be deeply spiritual

Likes
- Radio
- Concerts
- Record collecting
- Making music and singing
- Writing songs or music
- 'Working out' to music
- Relaxing to music

Learning activities for musical intelligence

- Using music to relax before learning
- Studying to music that reflects what is being learnt
- Reading rhythmically
- Writing a song, jingle, rap, poem, rhyme to carry out classroom tasks
- Using musical approaches to memorise key words

Naturalistic intelligence

Used for making sense of the natural world

An individual with well-developed **naturalistic** intelligence tends to have the following characteristics and likes:

Characteristics
- Good at identifying and classifying wildlife
- Can remember where different types of plants and animals live
- Is comfortable in different types of environment
- Attuned to the natural environment
- Troubled by pollution

Likes
- The outdoors
- Being close to wild animals and plants
- Observing and identifying wildlife
- Exploring and expeditions

Learning activities for naturalistic intelligence

- Learning outdoors, eg: on field trips
- Investigating into environmental issues
- Identifying and classifying exercises
- Reading about nature and the environment
- Listening to guest speakers who are nature specialists
- Devising plays or videos with environmental themes
- Studying the habits of school pets

Visual spatial intelligence

Used for visualisation and art

An individual with well-developed **visual spatial** intelligence tends to have the following characteristics and likes:

Characteristics
- Thinks and remembers in pictures
- Good sense of imaging/use of mind's eye
- Strong sense of colour
- Good at art/drawing
- Uses maps, charts and diagrams easily
- Good sense of direction
- Well dressed

Likes
- Film and video
- Posters and pictures
- Drawing, painting and sculpting
- Doodling
- Colour
- Making and wearing clothes
- Photography

Learning activities for visual spatial intelligence

- Learning from film, video, slides, PowerPoint presentations
- Using mind-maps, symbols and diagrams
- Designing and producing a poster with key facts
- Highlighting key points in different colours
- When reading, visualising events in the mind's eye
- Using visualisation
- Studying in different settings or areas of the room to gain a different perspective
- Converting information into diagrams or pictures

The text on multiple intelligences on the previous pages is adapted from *The Learner's Pocketbook* by Paul Hayden.

Emotional intelligence

Daniel Goleman introduced the concept of **emotional intelligence**, which builds on Gardner's inter- and intra-personal intelligences. Emotional intelligence includes:

- Self-awareness
- Self-discipline
- Persistence
- Empathy

Goleman reported on results of studies on Harvard students which measured their IQ and emotional intelligence, including an assessment of their ability to empathise, as well as their communication skills. The students were tracked into employment after they graduated and those who were earning the most were the ones whose ratings for emotional intelligence were higher, not those with the highest IQs*.

Although we would not want only to measure people's success by their earning power, this important research helped us to understand that emotional intelligence can be very important in determining success. What is exciting is that you can actively **teach** emotional intelligence.

Source: Goleman (1996)

Emotional intelligence in the classroom

You should try to develop better **emotional intelligence** in your students.
Consider the following methods:

- Try to develop better **communication skills** through discussion, debate and role play
- Help them distinguish between **thoughts** and **feelings**
- Emphasise the importance of **negotiation**
- Encourage each student to **value and respect** the opinions of others
- Ask students from time-to-time to consider something from **another person's point of view**
- Don't **judge**, **control** or **criticize** others
- Encourage students to value **reflection** as a means of improving themselves and their work

As you teach your subject try to incorporate these principles and model them in your own behaviour. They should complement your PSHE and citizenship programmes very well.

More multiple intelligences

Howard Gardner's theory sparked a lot of new interest in how human intelligence can be classified. A further two types of intelligence have been suggested by academics more recently:

- **Spiritual intelligence** – used to understand the spiritual dimension
- **Existential intelligence** – used to explore big questions about life and the universe

No doubt as the study of this fascinating field continues, still further types of intelligence will be proposed.

How many types of intelligence do you recognise in your classroom?

Thinking skills

There has been something of a revolution in the teaching of **thinking** in schools in England in the last few years. This has resulted from:

- Highly successful studies showing how subject-specific thinking skills programmes such as CASE (see page 93) can improve performance
- Widespread acceptance by teachers that the National Curriculum is heavy on content, but very light on the kind of skills that will create lifelong learners
- Government backing for thinking skills and their introduction into the Key Stage 3 strategy

Thinking skills can **transform learning** and you should try to make them an integral part of your teaching.

Thinking skills in the National Curriculum

The following five thinking skills are now embedded in the National Curriculum:

Information-processing skills enable students to:
- Locate, collect and recall relevant information
- Interpret information to show they understand relevant concepts and ideas
- Analyse information, eg: sort, classify, sequence, compare and contrast
- Understand relationships, eg: part/whole relationships

Reasoning skills enable students to:
- Give reasons for opinions
- Draw inferences and make deductions
- Use precise language to explain what they think
- Make judgements and decisions informed by reasons or evidence

Enquiry skills enable students to:
- Ask relevant questions
- Pose and define problems
- Plan what to do and how to research
- Predict outcomes, test conclusions and improve ideas

Thinking skills in the National Curriculum
(cont'd)

Creative thinking skills enable students to:

- Generate and extend ideas
- Suggest possible hypotheses
- Be imaginative in their thinking
- Look for alternative innovative outcomes

Evaluation skills enable students to:

- Evaluate information they are given
- Judge the value of what they read, hear and do
- Develop criteria for judging the value of their own and others' work or ideas
- Have confidence in their own judgements

While using these thinking skills students focus on '**knowing how**', as well as '**knowing what**' – in this way they learn how to learn. They also use '**metacognition**' (thinking about thinking) to reflect on what was done and find alternative strategies for success

Cognitive acceleration programmes

Various highly effective teaching programmes have been developed which come under the umbrella of '**cognitive acceleration**' approaches. The first was the Cognitive Acceleration through Science Education (CASE) programme, developed by King's College, London and piloted in ten schools in the 1980s.

The programme used a set of activities called Thinking Science, designed to promote higher level thinking in year 7 and 8 pupils. At the end of the trial, students who had used the activities showed greater gains in cognitive development than a control group who did not use them. When followed through to their GCSEs three or four years later, those who had used the CASE activities performed significantly better than the controls in science, and also in maths and English.

Parallel programmes for other areas of the curriculum such as maths (CAME) and design and technology (CATE) have subsequently been developed. Cognitive acceleration is very much in sympathy with the principles of accelerated learning.

It is worth finding out about the current schemes available and signing up for a course.

Giving feedback

Feedback is essential if learners are to make good progress. Feedback can be in the form of verbal or written comments, as well as non-verbal body language.

Make sure the feedback you give:
- Is fair and consistent
- Aims to move the student on to the next level
- Emphasises what the individual **can** do as well as pointing out what they need to do to improve
- Where possible includes an indication of grade or level reached

Regular student **assessment** will provide ample opportunities for feedback to be given. This can be both **formative** (promoting future learning) and **summative** (to determine standard attainment at a particular time).

Getting students to **mark their own work** and look at other students' work which is of a higher quality is an excellent way for them to receive feedback, while at the same time learning how to improve.

Visual tools

Visual tools help students make sense of written or verbal information. They can also aid the planning and drafting process, as well as being an ideal way to develop thinking skills. Consider using the following visual tools with your students:

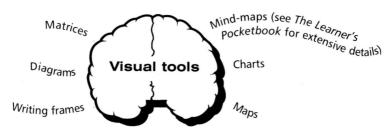

Matrices

Mind-maps (see *The Learner's Pocketbook* for extensive details)

Diagrams

Visual tools

Charts

Writing frames

Maps

An extremely useful lexicon of different visual tools was published in 2002 – *Thinking Skills and Eye-Que: visual tools for raising intelligence*, by Oliver Caviglioli, Ian Harris and Bill Tindall.

Logovisual thinking, a powerful technique and toolkit for visual thinking, has recently been introduced into classrooms (see website details on page 124).

High quality relationships

High quality **relationships** with your students should form the foundation of your work. You should not have become a teacher if you do not really like working with young people, so show your students that they are important to you. You can do this by:

- Valuing every individual
- Allowing students to have their say
- Asking students for their opinions
- Showing you care about their progress
- Showing an interest in their lives outside school
- Criticising behaviour not individuals
- Sorting out any disputes amicably
- Allowing students an 'escape route' if things go wrong
- Being prepared to compromise from time-to-time for the good of individuals
- Pointing out how students' successes or difficulties matter to you too

Valuing the opinions of students

Everyone is a **lifelong learner** and you should model this by accepting that you are continually learning how to become a better teacher. One of the most neglected sources of information in honing your teaching skills is the students themselves.

Make sure you:
- Let your students know you are learning too – it helps them to see the classroom as a learning environment for everybody
- Ask your students frequently what they enjoy and do not enjoy about your teaching, and how it can be improved further
- Are prepared to act on what they say to improve your teaching skills

Some teachers are reluctant to ask their students for such information, but time after time these concerns have been shown to be unfounded, and highly useful information has been gained on how teaching can be improved. Such work can also dramatically improve student-teacher relationships.

An example student questionnaire that will help you improve your teaching is included in the *Further Information* section.

Goal and target setting

Setting realistic **goals and targets** is important in motivating learners and getting successful results. Make sure your students' goals and targets are:

- **SMART** (**S**pecific, **M**easured, **A**chievable, **R**elevant, **T**ime-related)
- Set in line with ability
- Set by, or negotiated with, the individual concerned
- Recorded in a high-status document, such as a student record card
- Subject to periodic review
- Discussed by the students in their parental review meetings

Visualisation

Top performers in sport and the performing arts routinely use **visualisation** to help them be successful. The value of visualisation in education settings is now beginning to be recognised.

The most common form of visualisation involves an individual seeing themselves in their mind's-eye carrying out a skill or task to a very high level of competence. The individual invokes all the senses to make this as real an experience as possible. This 'mental rehearsal' has been shown to improve performance in many fields.

Visualisation

Visualisation is a relatively new concept within education, but your students may be able to use it to help them:

- Improve their performance in examinations by reducing levels of anxiety
- Overcome certain barriers to learning which are becoming blocks to progress, such as lack of confidence
- Achieve the best results by trying to visualise what high quality work looks like

Building self-esteem

Students with high **self-esteem** perform better and are better learners than those whose self-esteem is fragile. Try to build individuals' self-esteem by:

- Using frequent **praise** – students thrive on it
- Providing **rewards** and public commendations for excellent effort or achievement
- Carrying out specific **activities** designed to promote the building of self-esteem, such as personal affirmations
- Devising a class **identity** through the use of a song, rap or slogan, which individuals can relate to, and associate themselves with

Celebrating achievements

Take every opportunity to **celebrate the achievements** and successes of your students by:

- **Displaying** students' work prominently on your classroom walls and in corridor displays

- Getting coverage in your **local newspaper** of particularly noteworthy achievements

- Having a well-earned **celebration** at the end of each term – a Christmas party, quiz or event

Teaching your students how to learn

It is vital that your students acquire **learning skills** so they can learn effectively throughout their lives. You can promote learning skills in your classroom by:

- Teaching your students about their brains, learning and memory
- Emphasising the importance of study techniques such as mind-mapping and memory systems
- Encouraging your students to find out about their preferred learning styles and multiple intelligences
- Modelling good practice in your own work

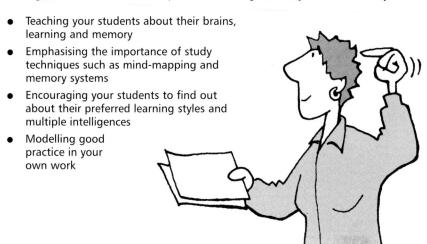

Notes

Introduction

 Getting your
Students Ready
to Learn

 Creating the
Right
Environment

 Teaching
Strategies

 Self-evaluation
Framework ◀

 Further
Information

A Self-evaluation Framework

Introduction to the framework

The **self-evaluation framework** on the following pages will help you to judge
the extent to which you use the accelerated learning principles described in this book
in your classroom. It will also provide you with a baseline on which to plan future
actions, which can be reviewed within an appropriate timescale. This will allow you
to prepare your own **accelerated learning action plan**.

How to use the self-evaluation
1. Work through it by reading the questions and score yourself by ticking the
    appropriate box according to the following key (work in pencil at this stage):

    0 = You feel you have not begun to address the question
    1 = You have started work, but it is in its early stages
    2 = You feel quite confident about the work you have done in this area
    3 = You feel the work you have done in this area represents excellent practice

2. As you do so note down any **action points** or issues that come to mind – this can
    form the basis of your action plan for improving your department.

Introduction to the framework

3. Then **add up** the scores for each section and for the self-evaluation as a whole, working out percentage scores as you do so. This will give you a **quantitative** assessment of the areas of your classroom practice that need to be developed.

4. Make a photocopy of the self-evaluation framework so you can refer back to it in future. You can carry out the exercise again in six or twelve months' time to judge the progress you have made.

5. Use the self-evaluation to identify the steps you need to take to become advanced at using the accelerated learning principles. This is your **accelerated learning action plan** which you should attach to the photocopy of your self-evaluation. Include in the plan a timeline for your actions and details of how other members of staff can help you achieve it.

Introduction to the framework

You should consider **sharing** the outcome of this self-evaluation with other members of your department and your senior management team. Its **quantitative** nature allows you to draw charts and graphs that will be helpful to you and others in making sense of the scores.

Note that your work to promote accelerated learning in your classroom will be much more effective if it is done with the support of the **senior management team** as part of a whole school approach. Find out what your school development plan says about teaching and learning, and consider what accelerated learning has to offer.

Your work on accelerated learning could be an important catalyst for whole school change in teaching and learning in your school. Find others on the staff who share your passion and work with them to try to get others to understand the benefits.

A self-evaluation framework

Preparing your students for learning	Emerging		Advanced	
	0	1	2	3
To what extent do you encourage your students to have a balanced diet that helps them learn?				
To what extent do you encourage your students to arrive at your lesson well hydrated?				
Do you help your students enter the alpha state at the start of your lessons?				
Do your students routinely set personal goals and targets for their learning?				
Do you help your students develop motivation for learning?				
Do you take active steps to reduce the stress levels of your students?				

Preparing your students score = ☐ /18 ☐ %

A self-evaluation framework

Preparing your classroom for learning	Emerging 0	1	Advanced 2	3
Is your classroom well oxygenated?				
Do you monitor the classroom temperature to keep it at an optimum level for learning?				
Do you ensure your classroom has appropriate levels of light for working?				
To what extent have you made your classroom a positive multi-sensory environment for learning?				
Have you used extensive displays of students' work in your classroom to celebrate their learning?				
Do you use flexible seating arrangements that complement the teaching style?				
Do you use nature (plants, etc.) to create a more pleasing environment for learning?				

Preparing your classroom score = ☐ /21   ☐ %

A self-evaluation framework

Creating a supportive environment	◁ Emerging		Advanced ▷	
	0	1	2	3
To what extent are high quality student-teacher relationships the foundation for your work?				
Do you expect high levels of commitment from every individual?				
Do you have clear classroom rules that have been negotiated with your students?				
How much do students have the chance to say what they expect from you as a teacher?				
Do you praise individuals and groups whenever possible?				
Do students understand their role in supporting the learning of others?				
Do you value students' achievements outside school?				
Do you use classroom displays of students' work to show examples of high quality work and excellent effort?				
Do you help students build their self-esteem?				
Do you find opportunities to develop emotional intelligence in your classroom?				

Creating a supportive environment score = ☐ /30   ☐ %

A self-evaluation framework

Teaching strategies	Emerging		Advanced	
	0	1	2	3
To what extent do you plan and deliver lessons according to a brain-friendly structure?				
How varied is your repertoire of teaching styles?				
Do you use open ended as well as closed questioning?				
Do you use thinking skills to improve learning opportunities?				
Is the learning broken down into achievable chunks?				
Do you give students choice over how a task is completed?				
Do you use knowledge of students' preferred learning styles to design inclusive activities?				
Do you use knowledge of students' intelligence profiles to design inclusive activities?				
Do you use knowledge of students' strengths and weaknesses in your subject area to design more meaningful tasks?				
Do you use target setting to give your students meaningful goals?				

A self-evaluation framework

Teaching strategies	Emerging 0	1	Advanced 2	3
Do your students know what they have to do to improve their performance in your subject area?				
Are you aware of any individual student's barriers to learning?				
Do you implement measures that will help individual students overcome their barriers to learning?				
Do you monitor these measures to judge their success?				
Do you provide plenty of opportunities for students to review their learning?				
Do you use homework effectively to extend learning beyond the classroom?				
Do you provide frequent oral and written feedback to students about their learning?				
Does your feedback balance positive support with suggestions for how to improve?				
Do you encourage students to mark their own work?				
Do you encourage your students to look at examples of work at different levels from their peers?				

A self-evaluation framework

Teaching strategies	Emerging		Advanced	
	0	1	2	3
Do you take brain breaks during learning?				
Do you use music to aid learning?				
Do you encourage your students to drink water as they learn?				
Do you display key words relating to specific topics being learnt?				
Do you use visual tools to promote learning?				
Are the materials you present to students accessible to each individual?				
Are the materials you present to students differentiated effectively?				
Do you use a wide variety of stimulus materials?				
Do you encourage your students to use visualisation to improve their performance?				

Teaching strategies score = ☐ /87   ☐ %

A self-evaluation framework

Helping your students learn how to learn	Emerging 0	1	Advanced 2	3
Do you teach your students about their brains and how they can learn more effectively?				
Do your students know their preferred learning styles and intelligence profiles?				
Do your students know how their preferred learning styles and multiple intelligences affect their learning?				
Do you teach your students memory techniques so they can recall information readily in exams?				

Helping your students learn how to learn score = ⬜ /12   ⬜ %

A self-evaluation framework

Working with parents/carers	Emerging		Advanced	
	0	1	2	3
Do your students attend their review meetings with parents/carers?				
Do your students do much of the talking about their progress at the review meetings?				
Do you explain to parents/carers how they can create a positive learning environment at home?				
Do you encourage parents/carers to write comments to you in your students' homework diaries?				

Working with parents/carers score = | /12 | | % |

Introduction

 Getting your
Students Ready
to Learn

 Creating the
Right
Environment

 Teaching
Strategies

 Self-evaluation
Framework

 Further
Information

Further
Information

A brief history of accelerated learning

There have been numerous important milestones in the history of accelerated learning and its practical application in classrooms in the UK, as summarised below.

1950-1980 – Research by psychologists into memory and learning, notably **Dr Georgi Lazanov**, who applied the results to a method for language learning called **Suggestopaedia**. This was the first attempt to apply what later became known as accelerated learning to learning in a specific area.

1985 – Publication of **Colin Rose's** book *Accelerated Learning*, the first popular science book on the subject. Rose, a science journalist, put forward a jargon-free account of the principles of accelerated learning based on the work of Lazanov and others

1993 – Publication of **Howard Gardner's** book *Frames of Mind: the theory of multiple intelligences*, which revolutionised our understanding of intelligence and how it relates to learning

A brief history of accelerated learning

1996 – Publication of **Alistair Smith's** book *Accelerated Learning in the Classroom*, the first book on the subject aimed at teachers in the UK. This important work built on the principles outlined in Colin Rose's work and other books, and developed a practical approach for the classroom, called the **accelerated learning cycle**.

1990s – Enthusiastic uptake of accelerated learning in **schools** in the UK, many of which based their work on Alistair Smith's framework. During this time a number of new books on the subject appeared which presented the ideas to specific audiences.

2001 – Publication of *Creating An Accelerated Learning School*, an account of how a secondary school in England, **Cramlington Community High School** in Northumberland, managed to embed accelerated learning into every classroom. The school is widely recognised as the most advanced school in the country in its application of the principles of accelerated learning, and has been highly praised in a recent OFSTED inspection.

Student questionnaire

I need your views to help me become a better teacher. Please complete this sheet as fully and honestly as you can. You do not have to put your name on this sheet.

1. Over the last half-term (or unit of work) how much do you think you have learnt from my lessons?

   1, 2, 3, 4, 5, 6, 7, 8, 9, 10

   (circle the number that applies best, where 1 = very little and 10 = very much)

2. Over the last half-term how much have you enjoyed my lessons?

   1, 2, 3, 4, 5, 6, 7, 8, 9, 10

3. What do you enjoy about my lessons?

4. What do you not enjoy about my lessons?

5. Mention three things that I could do that would make me a better teacher.

Thank you very much for your help

◀ *Use this questionnaire with the students you teach to gain feedback on the quality of your teaching.*

The advantage of using a scale on some of the questions is that it generates quantitative data which can be analysed and graphed. After an initial questionnaire such as this has been used, a much more sophisticated one can be devised to ask about particular aspects of your teaching.

Organisations and companies

Alite
45 Wycombe End, Beaconsfield HP9 1LZ
Tel. 01494 671444
email: office@alite.co.uk
www.alite.co.uk
- The UK's leading training company for accelerated learning, with courses and conferences led by author Alistair Smith and his team of trainers.

Campaign for Learning
19 Buckingham Street, London WC2N 6EF
Tel. 020 7930 1111
email: campaign@campaign-for-learning.org.uk
www.campaign-for-learning.org.uk
- Leading champions for lifelong learning, this charity supports research into effective teaching and learning which is in sympathy with the principles of accelerated learning. Work is currently underway in 24 schools throughout England to develop a learning approach that will inspire students to become lifelong learners.

Organisations and companies (cont'd)

Society for Effective Affective Learning (SEAL)
37 Park Hall Road, London N2 9PT
Tel. 020 8365 3869 email: seal@seal.org.uk www.seal.org.uk

- Founded in 1983, SEAL acts as a bridge between the latest scientific understanding of how the brain works and how to put this into practice. It is a network of people united by a passion for learning and is in sympathy with the principles of accelerated learning. Members include researchers and authors as well as teachers. The society offers a regular journal and superb conferences with international speakers and workshops in a range of topics related to accelerated learning in schools.

University of the First Age (UFA)
Millennium Point, Curzon Street, Digbeth, Birmingham B4 7XG
Tel. 0121 202 2347 email: marilyn_o'neil@birmingham.gov.uk www.ufa.org.uk

- An organisation dedicated to introducing the principles of accelerated learning into schools through out-of-hours activities. Since 1996 the UFA has run outstanding summer schools in a number of LEAs, which are now part of a fellowship programme that includes Super Learning Days and a variety of other benefits.

Books

Bransford, J.D., Brown, A. L. and Cocking, R. R. eds (2000) *How People Learn: brain, mind, experience and school*. National Academy Press.

Caviglioli, O., Harris, I. and Tindall, B. (2002) *Thinking Skills and Eye-Que: visual tools for raising intelligence*. Network Educational Press.

Dryden, G. and Vos, J. (2001) *The Learning Revolution*. Network Educational Press.

Gardner, H. (1993) *Frames of Mind: the theory of multiple intelligences*. Bloomsbury.

Goleman, D. (1996) *Emotional Intelligence: why it can matter more than IQ*. Bloomsbury.

Hayden, P. (1995) *The Learner's Pocketbook*. Management Pocketbooks.

Kyriacou. C. (1997) *Effective Teaching in Schools*. Nelson Thornes.

Jenson, E. (1995) *The Learning Brain*. Turning Point Publishing.

Rose, C. (1985) *Accelerated Learning*. Accelerated Learning Systems Ltd.

Smith, A. (1998) *Accelerated Learning in Practice*. Network Educational Press.

Smith, A. (2002) *The Brain's Behind It: new knowledge about the brain and learning*. Network Educational Press.

Smith, A. and Call, N. (1999) *The ALPS Approach: accelerated learning in primary schools*. Network Educational Press

Smith, A., Lovatt, M. and Wise, D. (2003) *Accelerated Learning: a user's guide*. Network Educational Press.

Wise, D. and Lovatt, M. (2001) *Creating An Accelerated Learning School*. Network Educational Press.

Websites

Accelerated Learning Centre (distributes books on accelerated learning)
www.accerelated-learning.co.uk

Accelerated Learning Systems www.acceleratedlearning.com

Brainwise www.brainwise.co.uk

BrainGym www.braingym.org

CASE (Cognitive Acceleration through Science Education)
www.kcl.ac.uk/depsta/education/teaching/CASE.html

CHAMPS (online/CD-ROM learning to learn course) www.learntolearn.org

Logovisual Thinking www.changeandinnovation.com/education

International Alliance for Learning www.ialearn.org

Network Educational Press Ltd (publishers of books and providers of consultancy
and training in accelerated learning) www.networkpress.co.uk

Model Learning (mind-mapping courses) www.modellearning.com

Teaching Thinking www.teachingthinking.net

21st Century Learning Initiative www.21learn.org

About the author

Brin Best

Brin Best BSc, PGCE, FRGS, FMA, MCIJ is managing director of Innovation *for* Education Ltd, an education training, publishing and consultancy company based in Yorkshire. He has fulfilled a wide variety of roles within education, including classroom teacher, college lecturer, head of department, school development officer and LEA advisory teacher. He writes and speaks widely on education issues and has a special interest in teaching and learning. He is carrying out a part-time PhD into accelerated learning at Leeds University. Whilst a teacher his department and students received numerous national awards for their work, and in 2000 he received a Millennium Fellowship for his pioneering work on environmental education. Brin is also the series consultant for the *Teachers' Pocketbooks* Series.

He can be contacted at:
Innovation *for* Education Ltd, 6 Manor Square, Otley, LS21 3AP.
Tel. +44 (0) 1943 466994   Fax +44 (0) 1943 465550
office@innovation4education.co.uk
www.innovation4education.co.uk

Acknowledgements

I am grateful to the staff and students of Settle High School & Community College who allowed me to explore the boundaries of accelerated learning while I was a teacher and head of department there.

I am also grateful to Paul Hayden for permission to base the pages on multiple intelligences and learning styles on material that first appeared in his excellent *The Learner's Pocketbook*.

The Learner's Pocketbook is one of more than 60 titles in the Management Series of Pocketbooks. For a full list see www.pocketbook.co.uk or call the publisher for a catalogue (Freephone 0800 028 6217 for U.K. callers).

Order Form

Your details

Name _____

Position _____

School _____

Address _____

_____

_____

Telephone _____

Fax _____

E-mail _____

VAT No. (EC only) _____

Your Order Ref _____

Please send me:

		No. copies
Accelerated Learning _____	Pocketbook	☐
_____	Pocketbook	☐
_____	Pocketbook	☐
_____	Pocketbook	☐
_____	Pocketbook	☐

Order by Post

Teachers' Pocketbooks

Laurel House, Station Approach
Alresford, Hants. SO24 9JH UK

Order by Phone, Fax or Internet

Telephone: +44 (0)1962 735573
Facsimile: +44 (0)1962 733637
E-mail: sales@teacherspocketbooks.co.uk
Web: www.teacherspocketbooks.co.uk

Pocketbooks

Teachers' Titles:

A-Z of Educational Terms
Accelerated Learning
Behaviour Management
Creative Teaching
Dyslexia
Form Tutor's
Fundraising for Schools

Head of Department's
ICT in the Classroom
Inclusion
Learning to Learn
Managing Workload
Mentoring in Schools
Primary Headteacher's
Primary Teacher's
Promoting Your School
Secondary Teacher's
Stop Bullying
Teaching Assistant's
Trips & Visits

Selected Management Titles:

Appraisals
Assertiveness
Career Transition
Challenger's
Coaching
Communicator's
Controlling Absenteeism
Decision-making
Developing People
Discipline
Emotional Intelligence
Empowerment
Energy & Well-being
Facilitator's
Icebreakers
Impact & Presence
Influencing
Interviewer's
Leadership
Learner's
Managing Budgets
Managing Change

Managing Your Appraisal
Meetings
Mentoring
Motivation
Negotiator's
NLP
People Manager's
Performance Management
Personal Success
Positive Mental Attitude
Presentations
Problem Behaviour
Project Management
Resolving Conflict
Succeeding at Interviews
Self-managed Development
Stress
Teamworking
Thinker's
Time Management
Trainer's
Vocal Skills